LIVING LEGENDS OF SPORTS

MARIA SHARAPOVA
TENNIS GRAND SLAM CHAMPION

JASON PORTERFIELD

Britannica Educational Publishing
IN ASSOCIATION WITH
ROSEN
EDUCATIONAL SERVICES

Published in 2019 by Britannica Educational Publishing (a trademark of Encyclopædia Britannica, Inc.) in association with The Rosen Publishing Group, Inc.
29 East 21st Street, New York, NY 10010

Distributed exclusively by Rosen Publishing.
To see additional Britannica Educational Publishing titles, go to rosenpublishing.com.

First Edition

Britannica Educational Publishing
J.E. Luebering: Executive Director, Core Editorial
Andrea R. Field: Managing Editor, Compton's by Britannica

Rosen Publishing
Kathy Kuhtz Campbell: Senior Editor
Nicole Russo-Duca: Series Designer and Book Layout
Cindy Reiman: Photography Manager
Sherri Jackson: Photo Researcher

Library of Congress Cataloging-in-Publication Data

Names: Porterfield, Jason, author.
Title: Maria Sharapova : tennis Grand Slam champion / Jason Porterfield.
Description: First Edition. | New York: Britannica Educational Publishing, in Association with Rosen Educational Services, 2019. | Series: Living legends of Sports | Includes bibliographical references and index. | Audience: Grades 5–8.
Identifiers: LCCN 2018014215| ISBN 9781508106371 (library bound) | ISBN 9781508106364 (paperback)
Subjects: LCSH: Sharapova, Maria, 1987—Juvenile literature. | Women tennis players—Russia (Federation)—Biography—Juvenile literature. | Internationaux de France de tennis, Roland Garros—History—Juvenile literature. | Australian Open (Tennis tournament)—History—Juvenile literature. | Wimbledon Championships—History—Juvenile literature.
Classification: LCC GV994.S47 P67 2019 | DDC 796.342092 [B] —dc23
LC record available at https://lccn.loc.gov/2018014215

Manufactured in the United States of America

Photo credits: Cover, p. 1 Lintao Zhang/Getty Images; back cover, p. 3 and interior pages (tennis court) Mykhailo Bokovan /Shutterstock.com; p. 5 Icon Sportswire/Getty Images; p. 7 SVF2/Universal Images Group/Getty Images; p. 8 Joe Scarnici /Getty Images; pp. 9, 10, 16 Professional Sport/Popperfoto/Getty Images; p. 12 Ken Levine/Getty Images; p. 14 Lutz Bongarts /Getty Images; p. 17 Michael Kienzler/Bongarts/Getty Images; p. 19 Jeff Gross/Getty Images; p. 20 Phil Cole/Getty Images; pp. 23, 29 Clive Brunskill/Getty Images; p. 24 Pool/Getty Images; p. 25 © AP Images; p. 26 Jasper Juinen/Getty Images; p. 27 Bloomberg/Getty Images; p. 33 Ilya S. Savenok/Getty Images; p. 35 Rob Kim/Getty Images; p. 36 Jemal Countess/WireImage /Getty Images; p. 37 Gladys Vega/Getty Images.

CONTENTS

Introduction 4

CHAPTER ONE Getting into the Game 6

CHAPTER TWO Education in Tennis 14

CHAPTER THREE Becoming the Best 22

CHAPTER FOUR Off the Court 32

Timeline 39

Other Living Legends of Tennis 41

Glossary 43

For More Information 45

Index 47

INTRO-DUCTION

Maria Sharapova surprised many tennis fans by gaining a spot to play in the 2017 US Open tournament. She had been suspended for more than a year following a positive test for the banned heart medication meldonium. In the months after returning from the suspension, she was still not ranked among the top 100 players in the world.

Sharapova had won the US Open before. She had been ranked number one in the world, yet she would still have to prove to the world that she belonged at the tournament. Her first opponent of the tournament was Simona Halep, who was seeded second in the tournament and ranked second in the world.

Sharapova won the first set of the match by a score of 6–4. Halep took the second set, 6–4. Sharapova played the third set with the dominating style that she had used throughout her career, winning by a score of 6–3. The win proved that she still belonged.

Maria Sharapova has demonstrated that kind of intensity since her early childhood in Russia, where she first picked up a secondhand racket and started hitting tennis balls. Her skill, determination, and ability to focus took her to Florida, where she trained at a famous tennis academy. She grew into one of the greatest players of the 21st century, winning some of the sport's most acclaimed tournaments and competing in the 2012 Summer Olympics in London, United Kingdom.

Sharapova has also been highly successful off the court. She has earned millions of dollars through endorsement deals with well-known companies and launched her own business. Sharapova has also been generous to several charities, giving to worthy causes throughout her career.

Maria Sharapova plays against Simona Halep on the first day of the 2017 US Open. It was Sharapova's first appearance in a Grand Slam tournament in over a year.

CHAPTER ONE

Getting into the Game

Maria Sharapova was born on April 19, 1987, in Nyagan, an industrial city in the Western Siberia region of Russia, which was part of the Soviet Union at the time. Her father, Yuri, and her mother, Yelena, were originally from a city called Gomel in present-day Belarus, which was also part of the Soviet Union. They had left Gomel in 1986, soon after a major disaster occurred at the Chernobyl nuclear power plant in nearby Ukraine. Like many residents of the area, they fled because they were afraid of exposure to radiation from the accident. They chose to go to Nyagan because Yelena's parents lived there.

Nyagan was a harsh place to live. The city was cold and had become grimy because of its many oil refineries and factories. Yuri worked in the region's oil fields, and Yelena stayed at home with young Maria. Maria's grandparents also helped take care of her.

QUICK FACT

Maria's real first name in Russian is Masha. Her family still calls her by that name.

Maria's family and others who lived near the Chernobyl nuclear power plant had to abandon their homes after the 1986 nuclear disaster. Many had to leave their belongings behind.

The family moved to the Russian resort town of Sochi when Maria was two years old. The climate was much better in Sochi than in Nyagan. Yuri worked around Sochi to support the family. Yelena stayed at home to take care of Maria.

Discovering Tennis

Shortly after the family moved to Sochi, Yuri Sharapov began playing tennis at a local park. He often took young Maria with him, and she would watch him play. One day when she was four years old she picked up his racket and started hitting balls. Yuri and the other adults were impressed by her ability to hit so well at such a young age. She showed that she had amazing coordination and an ability to concentrate.

Sharapova attends a 2014 event to mark the reopening of her hometown tennis court in Riviera Park in Sochi, Russia, where she first played the game.

Sochi native Yevgeny Kafelnikov plays at Wimbledon in 1994. Kafelnikov won the French Open in 1996 and the Australian Open in 1999. He thought young Maria had potential as a tennis player.

QUICK FACT

Child-sized tennis rackets were very had to find in Soviet Russia, so Maria had to use an adult-sized racket when she first started playing.

Soon, Maria started practicing with her father. They practiced regularly at a park near their home where some of Sochi's best tennis players played. Yuri made friends with the famous Russian tennis coach Yuri Yutkin. Yutkin offered to give Maria her first real tennis lesson. Like other adults who had seen her play, Yutkin was impressed by her speed and coordination.

Local tennis star Yevgeny Kafelnikov also saw that she had great promise. He gave her one of his rackets with a shortened handle that would be easier for her to use.

Maria continued to improve quickly. She could hit tennis balls consistently for hours, seemingly without tiring. By the time she was six, Yutkin already thought she could be a star.

Martina Navratilova plays in the 1993 US Open. That same year she saw Maria play at a tennis clinic and recommended that she go to the United States to train.

Picking Up Skills

Maria's parents believed that Yutkin was right. Maria was already well known among Sochi's tennis community. People often came by the park to watch her play.

Unfortunately, it was very expensive to move from Russia to the United States. Money was scarce for the Maria's family. But Yuri was determined to find a way to get Maria to the United States.

Maria's mother supported this dream, although she also encouraged Maria to have interests other than tennis. Yelena Sharapova had studied Russian literature in college and read many classic novels to her daughter. She inspired a love of reading in Maria and an appreciation for great books.

Maria's tennis skills continued to progress rapidly. In 1993, Yuri took his daughter to Moscow to participate in a tennis clinic. Maria would later write in her autobiography, *Unstoppable: My Life So Far*, that she barely remembers hitting at the clinic. But she made a strong impression on Martina Navratilova, a legendary tennis star who saw her play. Navratilova was so impressed by Maria's skills that she encouraged her parents to take her to the United States for training.

QUICK FACT

During her tennis career, Martina Navratilova won more singles titles than any other player since the Open era began in 1968.

Saving and Immigrating

Navratilova's comments made Yuri Sharapov more determined to help his daughter reach her potential as a tennis player. Yuri was able to get a visa to take Maria to the United States. Unfortunately, only one parent would be able to go with her. They decided that he would take Maria and that Yelena would follow later, when the family had enough money to afford the trip and it might be easier for her to get a visa.

Coach Rick Macci works with young Venus Williams in 1992. Two years later Macci took on Maria as a part-time student even though she was too young to enroll at his academy full-time.

Leaving Russia was expensive. Yuri had to borrow money for the trip. Finally, he and Maria left Russia. They arrived in Miami, Florida, in 1994. They had a small amount of luggage and $700 in cash. They did not know English.

Yuri took Maria to the Rick Macci Tennis Academy in Delray Beach, Florida. (In 1996, the academy moved to Boca Raton, Florida.) She tried out in front of some of the coaches. They were impressed, but she was too young to be accepted by the academy as a full-time student. Yuri and Maria also found a place to live. They rented a room in a small apartment that they shared with their landlord. Yuri worked odd jobs to pay their expenses. He also continued to coach her on courts near their new home.

CHAPTER TWO

Education in Tennis

In 1995, Maria's father enrolled her in the Nick Bollettieri Tennis Academy (part of the larger IMG Academy) in Bradenton, Florida. This academy was considered to be one of the best schools for young tennis players to develop into successful athletes. Maria's mother joined them in Florida in 1996, when she was finally able to get a visa and Yuri had saved enough to buy her a plane ticket.

Maria received most of her formal tennis training at the Nick Bollettieri Tennis Academy, where she spent her days working on different aspects of her game.

Academy Life

Life at the Nick Bollettieri Tennis Academy was challenging. Students were expected to do well in classes, practice their sport, and take part in competitions.

Many of the students who attended the academy came from families that were wealthy. Maria's family did not have much money. Maria was able to attend because she received a scholarship. She often felt out of place at the academy. She was small and thin for her age, and it was not unusual for her to lose her balance and fall down during practices and games. Many of her clothes were items that had been outgrown by the other girls at the academy because Maria's father could not afford to buy better things for her. She also struggled with speaking English early in her time there. Other girls bullied her for being different.

QUICK FACT

While she attended the Nick Bollettieri Tennis Academy, Maria had to live away from her family in a dormitory with other girls.

Maria was lonely at the academy, though her father had found an apartment a short distance away and often walked over to see her. She decided to stop worrying about the other girls. She dedicated herself to excelling at tennis. She developed an aggressive and dominating style of play. She learned how to use her powerful forehand swing to overwhelm her opponents. Maria did not like to play close to the net, so she worked on playing near the baselines at the back of the court. She developed a strong backhand swing to go with the forehand.

QUICK FACT

Maria taught herself English by watching cartoons on TV and looking at picture books. Her favorite books featured the heroine Pippi Longstocking.

Even as a young player, Maria overwhelmed opponents with her powerful forehand stroke. Here, her tough style is on display during a girls' singles match at the 2002 Austalian Open Junior Championships.

QUICK FACT

Maria signed her first sponsorship deal with the athletic shoe and clothing company Nike in 2000.

Early Competitions

Maria entered her first competition in 2000, playing in the Eddie Herr International Junior Tennis Championships in the girls' 16 division. More than 2,000 junior tennis players from more than 90 countries participate in the event each year. The event has served as a launching pad for many young players to take the next big step toward becoming professionals. Other tennis stars who first became famous by playing in the tournament include Roger Federer, Anna Kournikova, and Andy Roddick.

Russian tennis star Anna Kournikova is among the players whose careers received an early boost after playing in the Eddie Herr International Junior Tennis Championships.

Maria won her division. She beat her opponent, Myrian Casanova, in the final match in two sets. Maria had played so well that she was given the tournament's Rising Star Award. She was only 13 years old.

Continued success did not come easily. She began growing quickly and became more awkward on the court. It was hard for her to get used to her new height. She would eventually reach a full height of 6 feet 2 inches. The clumsiness affected her play and she went through a long losing streak at tournaments.

QUICK FACT

Although she left the Nick Bollettieri Tennis Academy without completing her high school education, Maria continued to do schoolwork. She earned her high school diploma online through Keystone High School.

Losing just made Maria more determined to find a way to start succeeding again. She kept playing an aggressive style of tennis and making adjustments. She changed her serve and it became much stronger.

Maria played in her first professional tournament in 2001 at age 14. It was an International Tennis Federation (ITF) Pro Circuit event in Bradenton, Florida. She lost her first-round match. But she went on to win several tournaments that year on the ITF Junior Circuit, even though she played mostly against older girls.

Maria also made a name for herself in some of the ITF's Junior Grand Slam tournaments. In September 2001, she made it to the second round of the US Open Junior Championships. In 2002, she was the runner-up in the Australian Open Junior Championships and the Junior Championships, Wimbledon.

QUICK FACT

The International Tennis Federation (ITF) is the world governing body of tennis. It holds Junior Circuit tournaments for players aged 18 and under. Its Pro Circuit tournaments are a training ground for players who hope to make it to the top level of professional tennis—the Women's Tennis Association (WTA) for women or the Association of Tennis Professionals (ATP) for men.

During this period, Maria also began playing more tournaments on the ITF Pro Circuit. She won her first Pro Circuit event in April 2002 in Gunma, Japan. Later that year, she won ITF tournaments in Vancouver, Canada, and Peachtree City, Georgia.

Maria stepped up to the next level when she entered her first Women's Tennis Association (WTA) tournament in March 2002. The WTA is the highest level of professional women's tennis. Still just 14 years old, she played in the Pacific Life Open in Indian Wells, California. Maria defeated Brie Rippner in her first match of the tournament. She then played against Monica Seles, who was one of the biggest stars in tennis at the time. Seles was 28 years old and had once been ranked first in the world. She was also someone Maria admired

Maria played well at the 2002 Pacific Life Open, although she lost to Monica Seles in two sets in the second round. Seles was ranked ninth at the time.

Playing at Wimbledon in 2003, Maria defeated 11th-seeded Jelena Dokic in the tournament's third round. Maria won the match in two sets by scores of 6–4 and 6–4.

QUICK FACT

The four tournaments that make up the Grand Slam of tennis are the Australian Open, the French Open, Wimbledon, and the US Open. They are the sport's most celebrated individual competitions.

greatly. Seles beat her easily, but the match showed Maria that she belonged among the best.

Sudden Success

Maria's big career breakthrough came in 2003. From that year on, she was one of the most dominant players in women's tennis. She entered the 2003 season ranked 189th in women's singles by the WTA. Her ranking was about to rise significantly.

Maria won her first WTA singles title at the Japan Open in 2003. She also made her debut in all four Grand Slam tournaments that year. Her best finish came at Wimbledon, where she advanced to the fourth round. Her biggest victory came when she beat Jelena Dokic in an upset win. Dokic was seeded 11th in the tournament. The victory was Sharapova's first over a top-20 player. She finished that year ranked 32nd in women's singles and 79th in doubles.

CHAPTER THREE

Becoming the Best

Sharapova continued her rapid rise through the upper ranks of women's tennis players. Her fierce style of play and the stories of her struggles growing up helped her build a global fan base. She had the full support of her parents. Her father was often at her matches. With her success, she could start supporting her parents.

New Milestones

Maria broke into the top 20 in the rankings for the first time in April 2004 after a strong performance in the Miami Open. She defeated a top-10 player for the first time in the Italian Open, beating 10th-ranked Elena Dementieva. She made it to the quarterfinals of a Grand Slam tournament for the first time in the French Open.

Her biggest moment of the year came in July, when she won her first Grand Slam title at Wimbledon. She was still fairly unknown when she entered the tournament. Sharapova surprised many tennis fans by beating former Wimbledon champion Lindsay Davenport in the semifinals. That win put her in the tournament finals against Serena Williams, who had won the tournament in 2002 and 2003.

Sharapova (*foreground*) defeated Serena Williams in two sets in the final round at Wimbledon in 2004 to win her first Grand Slam tournament.

QUICK FACT

Sharapova's victory at Wimbledon made her the first Russian tennis player to win that Grand Slam tournament.

Williams was the top seed in the tournament and was heavily favored to win. Instead, Sharapova beat her in two sets by scores of 6–1 and 6–4. That match marked the beginning of a rivalry that would last for years.

The Wimbledon championship title made her a star at age 17. "Maria Mania" began among fans, sportswriters, and advertisers. People were drawn to her because of her intense play, her good looks, and the story of her childhood.

Maria and her father, Yuri, pose with the trophy she was awarded for her 2004 Wimbledon victory.

Sharapova entered the top 10 in rankings after Wimbledon, jumping from 15th before the tournament to eighth after her victory. She went on to win the Korea Open and the Japan Open. Her last tournament of 2004 was the WTA Tour Championships, held that November. Sharapova made it to the finals and once again faced Serena Williams, whom she beat in three sets after losing the first set.

Sharapova finished the season as one of the biggest stars in tennis. She was ranked fourth in the world. Her hard work on the court paid off in other ways as well. Her tournament victories came with prize money. She could afford to take care of her parents.

Sharapova stands alongside tennis legend Billie Jean King with a giant replica of the check for $1 million that she received for winning the 2004 WTA Tour Championships.

Sustained Success

Sharapova's success continued for the next three years. She finished in the top five in the WTA rankings each year in 2005, 2006, and 2007. She became the number-one player in the world for the first time in August 2005, at age 18. She stayed in the top 10 in rankings until 2009.

QUICK FACT

Sharapova was the fifth-youngest women's player to become number one, behind Martina Hingis, Monica Seles, Tracy Austin, and Steffi Graf.

Sharapova won her second Grand Slam title in 2006, defeating Justine Henin in the final match of that year's US Open. Leg and shoulder

Sharapova serves the ball to Justine Henin during the final match of the 2007 WTA Tour Championships. She lost the match to Henin in three sets.

injuries forced Sharapova to miss several tournaments in 2007, but she continued to play well. She was the runner-up in the 2007 Australian Open, losing to Serena Williams. After that tournament, she was ranked number one for seven weeks. She was also the runner-up in the 2007 WTA Tour Championships, where she was beaten by Henin in three sets, 7–5, 5–7, and 3–6.

Sharapova's third Grand Slam title came the following year, when she won the 2008 Australian Open over Ana Ivanovic. She went on to win tournaments in Doha, Qatar, and Amelia Island, Florida. Sharapova regained the number-one ranking in May after the number-one player at the time, Henin, retired. But the rest of the season did not go well for Sharapova. She lost her number-one ranking after a disappointing performance in the French Open, where she was defeated in the fourth round. At Wimbledon in July, she failed to make it past the second round. Sharapova's season ended weeks later, when she had to withdraw from the 2008 Canada Masters. She had injured her right shoulder and would have to miss the rest of the season.

Stretching out, Sharapova returns the ball to Ana Ivanovic during the final match of the 2008 Australian Open. Sharapova prevailed in two sets, 7–5 and 6–3, to win her third Grand Slam title.

Surgery and Comeback

Sharapova had torn her rotator cuff, which is a group of tendons and muscles that surrounds the shoulder and keeps the arm in place. The injury required surgery and a long rehabilitation process.

Sharapova missed nine months of tournaments because of the injury and recovery. It forced her to miss the 2008 US Open and that year's Summer Olympics in Beijing, China, where she had planned to play for Russia. In May 2009, she fell out of the top 100 in the rankings for the first time since her debut.

Her serve had lost some of its power, but Sharapova quickly began working her way back. She returned to singles competition at the Warsaw Open in May 2009, reaching the quarterfinals. Then she made it to the quarterfinals of the French Open and did well in several smaller tournaments. She won the Pan Pacific Open in Tokyo, Japan, in September after her opponent, Jelena Jankovic, pulled out of the finals with an injury. By the end of the year, she was ranked 14th. Her comeback continued through 2010, when she won two minor tournaments and finished the year ranked 18th.

QUICK FACT

Sharapova is one of seven women to have a career Grand Slam in the Open era. That means she has won each of the four Grand Slam tournaments at least once.

The year 2011 marked Sharapova's full return from the shoulder injury. That year, she was the runner-up at Wimbledon to Petra Kvitova and won tournaments in Rome, Italy, and Cincinnati, Ohio. Her ranking again rose and she finished the season ranked fourth. She was the runner-up in the 2012 Australian Open, where she lost to Victoria Azarenka. Later that year, she won her fourth Grand Slam title by beating Sara Errani in the French Open. The victory gave her a rare career Grand Slam.

Holding the Coupe Suzanne Lenglen trophy, Sharapova celebrates her victory in the final match of the 2012 French Open against Sara Errani. The win gave Sharapova her fourth Grand Slam title.

Sharapova's ranking rose to number one again following her French Open victory. She competed in the 2012 Summer Olympics in London, United Kingdom, representing her home country of Russia. She made it to the finals, where her rival Serena Williams beat her in two sets by scores of 6–0 and 6–1. Sharapova took home a silver medal for finishing second. Sharapova was also the runner-up to Williams at the 2012 WTA Tour Championships. She finished the season ranked second.

The next three seasons were mixed for Sharapova. She was runner-up to Williams in the 2013 French Open. But hip and shoulder injuries forced her to miss several tournaments, including the US Open and the WTA Tour Championships. Sharapova finished the year ranked fourth.

She had another comeback year in 2014, when she won the French Open over Simona Halep for her fifth Grand Slam tournament victory. She also had victories in tournaments in Stuttgart, Germany; Madrid, Spain; and Beijing, China. She finished the year ranked second in the world. In 2015, she was the runner-up to Serena Williams at the Australian Open. She reached the semifinals at Wimbledon and the WTA Tour Championships.

By the end of 2015, Sharapova had won 35 women's singles titles in her career. Those successes came even as she battled injuries. She had won at least one singles title per year in every year between 2003 and 2015. That string of success was about to end.

Forced Away

Sharapova announced in March 2016 that she had failed a drug test at that year's Australian Open. She had tested positive for a drug called meldonium, which is a medication designed to treat several heart conditions. It can also improve an athlete's endurance and stamina. The drug was banned on January 1, 2016, by the World Anti-Doping Agency (WADA) after the agency saw increasing numbers of athletes apparently taking it to boost their performance.

Sharapova has said that she did not know at the time that the drug was banned, despite notices that had been sent out by the ITF. She also said that she had been prescribed the drug since 2006 to treat a magnesium deficiency and to correct an irregular heartbeat.

In June 2016, the ITF announced that Sharapova would be banned from the sport for two years. She appealed the ruling. The Court of Arbitration for Sport reduced the suspension to 15 months, dating back to January 2016.

The suspension cost her several valuable endorsement deals. It also cost her fans. She received little sympathy from them or from her fellow players.

Return to Play

Sharapova was ranked seventh in the world when the positive test was revealed. Her inactivity on the tour because of the ban caused her to lose her ranking. She was unranked when she became eligible to play again in April 2017. She won the first match of her return in the Porsche Tennis Grand Prix in Stuttgart, Germany, on April 26, 2017. However, she did not advance past the semifinals. In May, she played in the Madrid Open and the Italian Open. A leg injury forced Sharapova to leave the Italian Open, and she missed several tournaments with a left arm injury.

Sharapova gradually improved. She was able to participate in the US Open as a wild card that August. She beat the number two–ranked player at the time, Simona Halep, in the first round. She eventually lost in the round of 16 to Anastasija Sevastova. But her performance in the tournament was strong enough to boost her ranking from 146 to 103. By early October, she had climbed back into the top 100 for the first time since the suspension.

In October 2017, Sharapova won her 36th WTA title at the Tianjin Open in Tianjin, China. After this victory, her ranking jumped from 86 to 57. Sharapova finished 2017 ranked 59th and reentered the top 50 after reaching the semifinals in the Shenzhen Open in January 2018. She returned to the Australian Open in 2018, losing in the third round to Angelique Kerber. In June 2018, Sharapova lost in the quarterfinals of the French Open, but after the tournament her ranking rose to 23.

CHAPTER FOUR

Off the Court

Maria Sharapova's success on the court has led to many business and endorsement opportunities. She has also pursued work as a model and championed several charitable organizations. She is particularly drawn to children's charities and organizations that work to lessen the effects of the Chernobyl disaster.

Successful Spokesperson

Sharapova is a spokesperson for several recognizable brands. Going back to the days of "Maria Mania" after her 2004 Wimbledon victory, companies have wanted to be associated with her. Her major endorsement deals have included Nike, the luxury vehicle maker Porsche, the tennis racket manufacturer Head, and the bottled water company Evian.

Porsche and Nike briefly suspended their business relationships with Sharapova in response to her positive drug test in 2016 and the ban that followed. She lost other sponsors, including the luxury watchmaker Tag Heuer and the beauty products company Avon.

QUICK FACT

With her prize money and product endorsements, Sharapova was the top-earning female athlete for 11 years until Serena Williams overtook her in 2016, according to *Forbes* magazine.

In 2014, Sharapova poses with an issue of *SELF* magazine that features her on its cover. Her candy company, Sugarpova, held the special event at one of its stores in New York City.

Her role as the representative of several major companies has made her a familiar face in print magazines, in television commercials, and online. Clothing designers have taken note of her tall, lean frame, leading to a successful modeling career.

Time Away from Tennis

Sharapova remains very close to her parents. Her father has been a frequent presence at her matches. He has sometimes been criticized for coaching her from the stands. Her mother does not attend matches because she feels it is too stressful. Sharapova also has a strong connection to Russia. She has played on her home country's Olympics team and on its Fed Cup team. She is still a Russian citizen despite living in the United States since 1994.

Sharapova divides her time between her homes in Florida and California. She dated the Slovenian professional basketball player Sasha Vujacic from 2009 to 2012. The couple became engaged in 2010 before ending their relationship. Sharapova also dated the Bulgarian tennis player Grigor Dimitrov from 2013 to 2015. She has said in interviews that she would like to someday get married and have children.

QUICK FACT

Sharapova, who loves sweets, launched a candy company called Sugarpova in 2012.

When she's not playing tennis, Sharapova enjoys dancing and watching movies. Her favorite films include *Love Actually*, *Something's Gotta Give*, and *Mona Lisa Smile*. She enjoys Thai and Russian food and has held on to her love of reading from her childhood. She published an autobiography (written with Rich Cohen) titled *Unstoppable: My Life So Far* to positive reviews in 2017.

Sharapova visits a bookstore in New York City in 2017 to promote and sign copies of her memoir, *Unstoppable: My Life So Far*.

QUICK FACT

The Maria Sharapova Foundation Scholarship for Youth from the Chernobyl-Affected Areas of Belarus is a joint venture with the UNDP that provides scholarships for deserving students from that region.

Committed to Charity

Sharapova has dedicated her time to numerous charities throughout her career. She became a goodwill ambassador for the United Nations Development Programme (UNDP) in 2007. Through the program, she has worked on behalf of and raised money for Chernobyl-related organizations. She has supported efforts in the affected countries of Russia, Belarus, and the Ukraine. She traveled to Belarus in 2010 to meet with children and see the results of some of those projects, including a tennis center in Gomel.

In 2007, the associate administrator of the United Nations Development Programme (UNDP) presents Sharapova with a certificate making her a UNDP goodwill ambassador. The ceremony was held at the United Nations in New York City.

Over the course of her career, Sharapova has given to groups such as The Global Fund, Variety—The Children's Charity, and (RED). She auctioned off a Porsche Cayenne that she had won as a tournament prize at the 2004 WTA Tour Championships, raising more than $50,000 for the victims of a school hostage crisis in Beslan, Russia. She has also helped to raise money for victims of natural disasters in the United States and the Caribbean. She participated in an exhibition in 2004 in Tampa, Florida, to raise money for hurricane victims there. In October 2017, she visited Puerto Rico with tennis star and 2016 Olympic gold medalist Monica Puig to help with recovery from

Sharapova (*left*) and Olympic gold medalist Monica Puig (*at Sharapova's left*) hand out donated supplies to residents of Puerto Rico after Hurricane Maria devastated the island in October 2017.

Hurricane Maria. Sharapova donated the profits from her Sugarpova brand products for the rest of 2017 to the recovery efforts.

In March 2018, Sharapova announced the establishment of the Maria Sharapova Women's Entrepreneur Program, a partnership with the National Association of Women Business Owners. The program's team mentors businesswomen selected from across the United States for 12 months. It encourages the women in their entrepreneurial endeavors, offers them educational opportunities, and helps to fund their marketing and other business efforts.

TIMELINE

1987: Maria Sharapova is born on April 19 in Nyagan, Russia.

1989: Maria's family moves to the Russian resort city of Sochi, where Maria starts playing tennis around age four.

1993: Sharapova catches the attention of tennis star Martina Navratilova at a tennis clinic in Moscow.

1994: Maria Sharapova and her father, Yuri, move to Florida so that Maria can receive proper coaching.

1995: The Nick Bollettieri Tennis Academy gives Maria a scholarship.

1996: Maria's mother, Yelena, moves to the United States to be with her and her father.

2000: Maria wins the Eddie Herr International Junior Tennis Championships for girls younger than 16. Nike signs Sharapova to a sponsorship deal.

2001: Sharapova plays her first match as a professional.

2002: Sharapova plays in her first WTA tournament in Indian Wells, California. She wins her first ITF Pro Circuit tournament in Gunma, Japan.

2003: Sharapova plays in all four Grand Slam tournaments for the first time.

2004: Sharapova wins her first Grand Slam title at Wimbledon.

2005: Sharapova is ranked the number-one women's tennis player in the world for the first time.

2006: Sharapova wins her second Grand Slam title at the US Open.

2008: Sharapova wins her third Grand Slam title at the Australian Open. She tears her rotator cuff and misses several months of playing time because of the injury.

2012: Sharapova wins the French Open to complete her career Grand Slam. She wins a silver medal in women's tennis for Russia at the London Olympic Games. She forms her candy business, Sugarpova.

2014: Sharapova wins her fifth Grand Slam tournament at the French Open.

2016: Sharapova tests positive for a performance-enhancing drug and is suspended.

2017: Sharapova returns to professional tennis in April after her suspension ends. She travels to Puerto Rico in October to help recovery efforts following Hurricane Maria.

2018: Sharapova reenters the top 50 in the WTA rankings. She announces the creation of the Maria Sharapova Women's Entrepreneur Program, a joint venture with the National Association of Women Business Owners. She ranks 23rd after making it to the quarterfinals at the French Open.

OTHER LIVING LEGENDS OF TENNIS

Billie Jean King (1943–) won 39 major titles in her tennis career, competing in both singles and doubles. She was perhaps the greatest woman doubles player in tennis history. She helped to organize the Women's Tennis Association and to establish a women's pro tour in the early 1970s. In a match billed as the Battle of the Sexes in 1973, King defeated Bobby Riggs, a former Wimbledon and US champion.

Chris Evert (1954–) was the first person to win 1,000 singles matches. Evert won a record seven French Open singles titles and six US Open singles titles (since tied by Serena Williams). She won 157 singles titles, 18 of which were Grand Slam events. She was ranked either number one or number two in the world from 1975 to 1986.

Martina Navratilova (1956–) was a dominant force in women's tennis in the 1970s and 1980s. Her 167 career singles titles are more than any other player has ever won. She finished her career with 59 Grand Slam titles, with 18 in singles play, 31 doubles, and 10 mixed doubles.

Monica Seles (1973–) won nine Grand Slam singles titles and held the WTA's number-one ranking at the end of 1991 and 1992. She missed more than two years after a spectator stabbed her in 1993, but she came back in 1995 and won the Australian Open in 1996. She won 53 career singles titles and a bronze medal at the 2000 Olympic Games in Sydney, Australia.

Venus Williams (1980–) has won 49 career singles titles in a professional career that dates back to 1994. In 2000 she became the first African American woman to win Wimbledon since Althea Gibson in 1958. She earned her first number-one ranking in 2002.

Roger Federer (1981–) is widely considered one of the best men's players in history. He holds a career Grand Slam and has won 97 career singles titles, including a record 20 men's Grand Slam titles. He has spent more than 300 weeks ranked at number one, the most of any player in history.

Serena Williams (1981–) revolutionized women's tennis with her powerful style of play. Since making her professional debut in 1995, she has won 72 career singles titles, including a record 23 Grand Slam singles titles. She has also won 23 doubles titles, all but one playing alongside her sister, Venus Williams. Serena Williams holds a career Grand Slam.

Rafael Nadal (1986–) made his professional debut in 2001. He is one of only five men to win a career Grand Slam in the Open era. By mid-2018 he had won 79 tournament titles, including 17 Grand Slam titles.

Caroline Wozniacki (1990–) made her professional debut in 2005. She earned her first number-one ranking in 2010. In the 2009 US Open finals, she became the first Danish person to reach a Grand Slam final. Her victory at the 2018 Australian Open was her 28th WTA singles title overall.

Simona Halep (1991–) played her first professional events in her native Romania in 2006. She won her first six WTA titles in 2013 and over the next few years reached the finals at the French Open, the Australian Open, and the WTA Tour Championships. Halep won her 17th WTA singles title and first Grand Slam tournament at the French Open in June 2018.

GLOSSARY

academy A high school or college in which special subjects or skills are taught.

backhand A stroke (as in tennis) made with the back of the hand turned in the direction of movement.

baseline A boundary line at either end of a court (as in tennis or basketball).

coordination The ability to move different parts of the body together well or easily.

deficiency A shortage of substances necessary to health.

dominating Having a commanding position or controlling power over someone or something.

endorsement deal An agreement to advertise a product or service.

forehand A stroke (as in tennis) made with the palm of the hand turned in the direction in which the hand is moving.

Grand Slam A series of major tennis tournaments (Australian Open, French Open, Wimbledon, and US Open) held each year.

hostage A person held captive by someone who demands that certain terms be met before the captured person is freed.

industrial Having a lot of manufacturing activities.

meldonium A prescription medicine sometimes misused by athletes to boost performance.

nuclear power plant A facility that uses nuclear reactions to produce electricity.

radiation A type of dangerous and powerful energy that is produced by nuclear reactions.

rehabilitation The process of restoring a person to a condition of health.

rotator cuff A supporting and strengthening structure of the shoulder joint.

scholarship Money given (as by a college) to a student to help pay for further education.

seed To give a player a rank that shows how likely that person is to win a competition.

serve To put the ball in play (in tennis).

set A division of a tennis match won by the side that wins at least six games beating the opponent by two games or by winning a tiebreaker. A series of games makes up a set, and a series of sets makes up a match.

stamina Endurance, especially during exercise.

tournament A series of games or contests that make up a single unit of competition.

visa A mark made on a passport that is a sign of approval and permission for the traveler to proceed.

wild card In professional tennis, an invitation to a tournament for a player who does not qualify based on ranking.

FOR MORE INFORMATION

Books

Bildner, Phil. *Martina & Chrissie: The Greatest Rivalry in the History of Sports*. Somerville, MA: Candlewick Press, 2017.

Gifford, Clive. *Tennis*. London, UK: Franklin Watts, 2017.

Gitlin, Marty. *Wimbledon*. Minneapolis, MN: ABDO Publishing, 2013.

Hall, Brian. *Pioneers in Women's Sports*. Minneapolis, MN: SportsZone, 2018.

Hanold, Maylon. *Women in Sports: A Reference Handbook*. Santa Barbara, CA: ABC-CLIO, 2018.

Luke, Andrew. *Tennis*. Broomall, PA: Mason Crest Publishers, 2017.

Mallick, Nita. *Tennis: Girls Rocking It*. New York, NY: Rosen Publishing, 2016.

Mooney, Carla. *Tennis*. Detroit, MI: Lucent Books, 2013.

Peters, Stephanie True. *Serena Williams*. New York, NY: Little, Brown and Company, 2017.

Rissman, Rebecca. *The Chernobyl Disaster*. Minneapolis, MN: ABDO Publishing Company, 2014.

Savage, Jeff. *Maria Sharapova*. Rev. ed. Minneapolis, MN: Lerner Publications, 2014.

Shoup, Kate. *Billie Jean King: The Battle of the Sexes and Title IX*. New York, NY: Cavendish Square, 2016.

Stanmyer, Jackie. *Althea Gibson and Arthur Ashe: Breaking Down Tennis's Color Barrier*. New York, NY: Cavendish Square, 2016.

Yomtov, Nelson. *Russia*. New York, NY: Children's Press, 2013.

Zuckerman, Gregory, with Gabriel and Elijah Zuckerman. *Rising Above: Inspiring Women in Sports*. New York, NY: Philomel Books, 2018.

Websites

International Tennis Hall of Fame
https://www.tennisfame.com

Maria Sharapova Official Website
http://www.mariasharapova.com

Women's Tennis Association
http://www.wtatennis.com

INDEX

A

Austin, Tracy, 25
Australian Open, 20, 27, 28, 30, 31
Australian Open Junior Championships, 18
Azarenka, Victoria, 28

B

backhand swing, 15
banned substances, 4, 30, 32
Bradenton, Florida, 14, 18

C

Canada Masters, 27
Casanova, Myrian, 17
charity work, 4, 32, 36–38
Chernobyl, 6, 32, 36

D

Davenport, Lindsay, 22
Delray Beach, Florida, 13
Dementieva, Elena, 22
Dokic, Jelena, 21

E

Eddie Herr International Junior Tennis Championships, 16
endorsements, 4, 31, 32
Errani, Sara, 28

F

Federer, Roger, 16
forehand swing, 15
French Open, 20, 22, 27, 28, 30, 31

G

Graf, Steffi, 25

H

Halep, Simona, 4, 30, 31
height, 17, 34
Henin, Justine, 25, 27
Hingis, Martina, 25

I

injuries, 27, 28, 30, 31
International Tennis Federation (ITF), 18, 30, 31
Italian Open, 22, 31
Ivanovic, Ana, 27

J

Jankovic, Jelena, 28
Japan Open, 21, 24

K

Kafelnikov, Yevgeny, 9
Keystone High School, 17
Korea Open, 24
Kournikova, Anna, 16
Kvitova, Petra, 28

M

Maria Sharapova Women's Entrepreneur Program, 38
Maria Sharapova Foundation Scholarship for Youth from the Chernobyl-Affected

Areas of Belarus, 36
meldonium, 4, 30
Miami Open, 22
modeling, 32, 34

N

Navratilova, Martina, 11
Nick Bollettieri Tennis Academy, 14, 15, 17
Nike, 16, 32
Nyagan, Russia, 6, 8

O

Olympic Games, 4, 28, 30, 34

P

Pacific Life Open, 18
Pan Pacific Open, 28
Pippi Longstocking, 15

R

reading, 11, 34
Rick Macci Tennis Academy, 13
Rippner, Brie, 18
Rising Star Award, 17
Roddick, Andy, 16
rotator cuff, 28

S

scholarship, 15
Seles, Monica, 18, 20, 25
Sharapov, Yuri (father), 6, 8, 9, 11, 13, 15, 22, 24, 34
Sharapova, Yelena (mother), 6, 8, 11, 14, 22, 24, 34
Sochi, Russia, 8
surgery, 28

U

United Nations Development Programme, 36
Unstoppable: My Life So Far, 11, 34
US Open, 4, 20, 25, 28, 30, 31
US Open Junior Championships, 18

W

Warsaw Open, 28
Williams, Serena, 22, 23, 24, 27, 30
Wimbledon, 20, 21, 22, 23, 24, 27, 28, 32
Wimbledon Junior Championships, 18
Women's Tennis Association (WTA), 18, 20, 21, 24, 25, 27, 30, 37

Y

Yutkin, Yuri, 9, 11